EVERY DAY THOUGHTS™

Thank God for
Sisters

new seasons®

New Seasons is a registered trademark of Publications International, Ltd.
Every Day Thoughts is a trademark of Publications International, Ltd.

© New Seasons®
All rights reserved.
This publication may not be reproduced in whole or in part
by any means whatsoever without written permission from:

Louis Weber, CEO
Publications International, Ltd.
7373 North Cicero Avenue
Lincolnwood, Illinois 60712

www.pilbooks.com

Permission is never granted for commercial purposes.

Manufactured in China.

8 7 6 5 4 3 2 1

ISBN-13: 978-1-4127-9998-0
ISBN-10: 1-4127-9998-8

TO: _____

FROM: _____

Original inspirations by Marie Jones, Lynda Twardowski, and Natalie Walker Whitlock.

Additional inspirations by Nancy Parker Brummet, Elaine Creasman, Lain Chroust Ehmann, Georgann Gouryeb-Freeman, Jan Goldberg, Judy Hershner, Barbara Briggs Morrow, Jennifer John Ouellette, Donna Shryer, June Stevenson, LeAnn Thieman, Kathryne Lee Tirrell, and Tricia Toney.

Quotations compiled by Joan Loshek.

Picture Credits
Front Cover: **Planet Art Collection**
Circa Art Collection; PhotoDisc Collection; Planet Art Collection; SuperStock: Bridgeman Art Library; John Bunker; Christie's Images; David David Gallery; Peter Harholdt; Elizabeth Barakah Hodges; Huntington Library; Hyacinth Manning; Anatoly Sapronenkov; Edmond Van Hoorick.

January 1

Sisters are miracles created by chance but sustained by love.

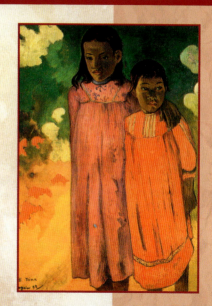

Acknowledgments

January 3; June 8; August 22; September 22; December 19: Excerpts from *Sisters* by Carol Saline. **January 10:** Excerpt from *Same Song, Separate Voices* by Peggy Lennon. Reprinted with permission from Peggy Lennon. **January 18:** Excerpt from "Violet Twilights" from *Love and Solitude* by Edith Södergran (Finland), translated by Stina Katchadourian. Reprinted with permission from Stina Katchadourian. **January 26; February 7; March 11; April 1:** Excerpts from *Mom Loves Me Best* by Linda Sunshine. © 2006 by Linda Sunshine. Reprinted with permission from Andrews McMeel Publishing. All rights reserved. **February 2:** Excerpt from *Welcome to Earth, Mom* © 1992 by Adair Lara. Reprinted with permission from Chronicle Books LLC, San Francisco. Visit ChronicleBooks.com. **April 30:** Excerpt from *Animal Dreams* by Barbara Kingsolver. © 1990 by Barbara Kingsolver. Reprinted with permission from HarperCollins Publishers. **June 2:** Excerpt from "Girl's-Eye View of Relatives" from *Times Three* by Phyllis McGinley. © 1959 by Phyllis McGinley. Reprinted with permission from Viking Penguin, a division of Penguin Group (USA), Inc. **June 21:** Excerpt from *Poustinia* by Catherine de Hueck Doherty. Reprinted with permission from Madonna House Publications, www.madonnahouse.org. **July 1:** Excerpt from "My Sister Dancing" by Elizabeth Jolley from *Sisters*, edited by Drusilla Modjeska. Reprinted with permission from HarperCollins Publishers Australia. **July 24; September 8; October 4:** Excerpts from *No Friend Like a Sister* by Barbara Alpert. © 1996 by Barbara Alpert. Reprinted with permission by Barbara Alpert. **August 1:** Excerpt from *Between Sisters* by Barbara Mathias. © 1992 by Barbara Mathias. Reprinted with permission from Barbara Mathias. **August 18:** Excerpt from *USA Weekend*, January 27–29, 1995. Reprinted with permission from Joyce Maynard, author of *At Home in the World*. **October 6:** Excerpt from "Sisters" by Irving Berlin. © 1953 by Irving Berlin. © Copyright renewed. International copyright secured. All rights reserved. Reprinted with permission. **October 9:** Excerpt from *Dear Octopus* by Dodie Smith. Reprinted with permission from the Literary Executor of the Estate of the Late Dodie Smith. **November 29:** Excerpt from *The Family of Man* (1955), courtesy the Museum of Modern Art, New York.

JANUARY 2

Good things become wonderful the moment I share them with my sister.

ANNIVERSARY GIFTS

	TRADITIONAL	MODERN		TRADITIONAL	MODERN
First	Paper	Clock	Twelfth	Silk & Linens	Pearls
Second	Cotton	China	Thirteenth	Lace	Textiles & Furs
Third	Leather	Crystal & Glass	Fourteenth	Ivory	Gold jewelry
Fourth	Fruit & Flowers	Appliances	Fifteenth	Crystal	Watch
Fifth	Woodenware	Silverware	Twentieth	China	Platinum
Sixth	Candy & Iron	Woodenware	Twenty-fifth	Silver	Silver
Seventh	Wood & Copper	Desk set	Thirtieth	Pearls	Diamond jewelry
Eighth	Bronze & Pottery	Linen & Lace	Thirty-fifth	Coral	Jade
Ninth	Pottery & Willow	Leather goods	Fortieth	Ruby	Ruby
Tenth	Tin & Aluminum	Diamond jewelry	Fiftieth	Gold	Gold
Eleventh	Steel	Jewelry	Sixtieth	Diamonds	Diamonds

January 3

I feel blessed to have two people in my life who have to take me as I am, whereas the world doesn't.

—Sandy Wasserstein

DECEMBER
BIRTHDAYS & ANNIVERSARIES

Birthstone: Turquoise
Flower: Poinsettia

January 4

Sisters share a bond that cannot be accounted for by blood and birth alone.

NOVEMBER
BIRTHDAYS & ANNIVERSARIES

Birthstone: Topaz
Flower: Chrysanthemum

JANUARY 5

Thank You, God

Thank God for sisters. They overlook our vices and celebrate our virtues.

OCTOBER
BIRTHDAYS & ANNIVERSARIES

Birthstone: Opal
Flower: Dahlia

JANUARY 6

Thank You, Sister

Growing up it sometimes felt like it was you and me against the world. Thank you for always choosing to stand beside me, in good times and in bad.

SEPTEMBER
BIRTHDAYS & ANNIVERSARIES

Birthstone: Sapphire
Flower: Aster

January 7

They say God couldn't be everywhere, so he created mothers. And when mothers couldn't be everywhere, he created sisters.

AUGUST
BIRTHDAYS & ANNIVERSARIES

_____   _____
_____   _____
_____   _____
_____   _____
_____   _____
_____   _____
_____   _____
_____   _____

Birthstone: Peridot
Flower: Gladiolus

January 8

Our relationship has had its ups and downs, but we never let anything come between us for long. We're not perfect; we're sisters.

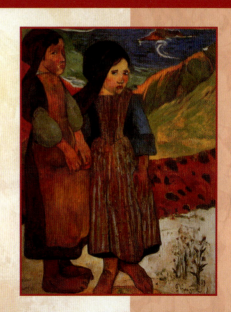

JULY

BIRTHDAYS & ANNIVERSARIES

_____   _____
_____   _____
_____   _____
_____   _____
_____   _____
_____   _____
_____   _____
_____   _____

Birthstone: Ruby
Flower: Sweet Pea

January 9

An older sister is like a guardian angel. A younger sister is like an angel-in-training. Lucky is the person who gets to have one of each.

JUNE
BIRTHDAYS & ANNIVERSARIES

Birthstone: Pearl
Flower: Rose

JANUARY 10

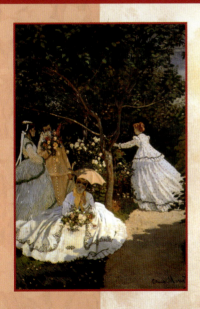

How do I feel about my sisters? They love me; they know me and they still love me.

—PEGGY LENNON,
SAME SONG, SEPARATE VOICES

MAY

BIRTHDAYS & ANNIVERSARIES

Birthstone: Emerald
Flower: Lily of the Valley

January 11

Sisters will always believe in you, even when you have stopped believing in yourself.

APRIL

BIRTHDAYS & ANNIVERSARIES

_____   _____

_____   _____

_____   _____

_____   _____

_____   _____

_____   _____

_____   _____

Birthstone: Diamond
Flower: Daisy or Lily

JANUARY 12

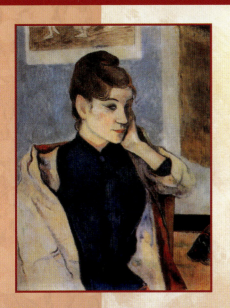

Thank You, Sister

They say it is the friends you can call at 4:00 A.M. who matter. You have always been that friend to me. Thank you.

MARCH
BIRTHDAYS & ANNIVERSARIES

_____   _____

_____   _____

_____   _____

_____   _____

_____   _____

_____   _____

_____   _____

_____   _____

Birthstone: Aquamarine
Flower: Violet

JANUARY 13

An ounce of blood is worth more than a pound of friendship.
—SPANISH SAYING

FEBRUARY
BIRTHDAYS & ANNIVERSARIES

Birthstone: Amethyst
Flower: Primrose

January 14

To the outside world we grow old. But to a sister, we have the same hands that played, the same eyes that smiled, and the same hearts that loved when we were young.

JANUARY
BIRTHDAYS & ANNIVERSARIES

Birthstone: Garnet
Flower: Carnation

January 15

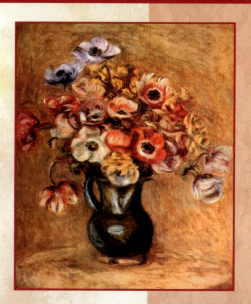

In the garden of my heart, Sister, you are the tallest, brightest, most beautiful flower of them all.

December 31

You can never lose your sister so long as you hold her tightly within your heart.

JANUARY 16

Thank You, God

Thank you, God, for the gift of sisterhood—
for the bonds we share, the joys we experience,
and the hardships we learn and grow from.
We are blessed to have each other.

DECEMBER 30

You must choose your friends wisely, but God chooses your sisters. Lucky for us, he is wiser than we could ever be.

January 17

Sisters are really moms, friends, and angels rolled up together in one perfectly proportioned package of sibling sweetness.

DECEMBER 29

I love that I never need to be careful with what I say to my sister—she always knows what I'm going to say before I say it.

January 18

Beautiful sisters, come high up to the strongest rocks,
we are all fighting women, heroines, horsewomen.

—Edith Södergran, "Violet Twilights"

DECEMBER 28

Thank You, Sister

I have learned from you what a big difference a little act can make.

JANUARY 19

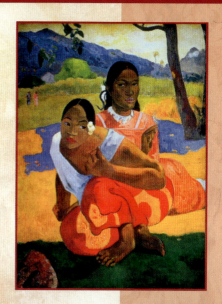

Sisters cherish each other as a mother does her child, but with a special reverence and respect that can exist only between equals.

December 27

Write your sister's weak points in the sand and her strong points in stone.

—Unknown

JANUARY 20

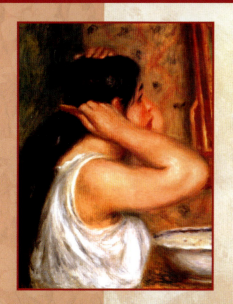

My sister sees me without makeup, with my hair undone, and in the grungiest of clothes... and she still thinks I'm beautiful.

December 26

My sister! My sweet sister! If a name
Dearer and purer were, it would be thine.

—Lord Byron, *Epistle to Augusta*

JANUARY 21

Sisters are like snowflakes—though there are many, each one is unique and special.

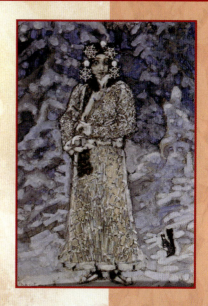

December 25

Whether she comes into your life at birth, or later through marriage, a true sister is a gift that keeps on giving.

JANUARY 22

You always listen
When I need an ear,
You comfort my heart and wipe my tear.
Your counsel is godly,
Full of wisdom and true,
I thank God for giving me a sister like you.

December 24

God presents the path.
A sister points out its possibilities.

January 23

Even if you weren't my sister,
I'd want you as a friend.

December 23

Sisters share the happy memories of the past, the joyful moments of the present, and the hope and promise of the future.

January 24

No one can—or would dare—tell you the truth like a sister.

DECEMBER 22

There can be no situation in life in which the conversation of my dear sister will not administer some comfort to me.

—LADY MARY WORTLEY MONTAGU

JANUARY 25

You should never look down on a sister except to pick her up.

—UNKNOWN

DECEMBER 21

When you're hurt, your sister feels your pain. When you're happy, she shares your joy.

JANUARY 26

If you don't understand how a woman could both love her sister dearly and want to wring her neck at the same time, then you were probably an only child.

—LINDA SUNSHINE, *MOM LOVES ME BEST (AND OTHER LIES YOU TOLD YOUR SISTER)*

December 20

A ministering angel shall my sister be.

—WILLIAM SHAKESPEARE, *Hamlet*

January 27

God gave us sisters for all the times when even the arms of angels aren't strong enough to hold us.

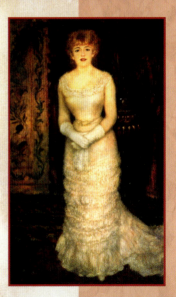

DECEMBER 19

My sisters have shown me how to live.
—GEORGETTE WASSERSTEIN

JANUARY 28

Sisters are always there,
no matter how much time
or distance lies between you.

December 18

Sisters are—
Angels who guide you,
Spirits who inspire you,
Warriors who defend you,
Guardians who protect you.

January 29

The definition of a family is the love, sweat, and tears shared through a lifetime together.

December 17

My sister is a precious reminder of who I am and where my roots are. She's a link between my present and my past.

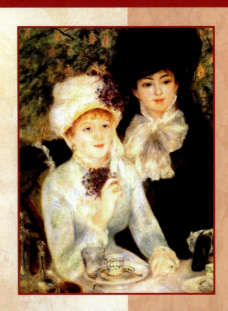

JANUARY 30

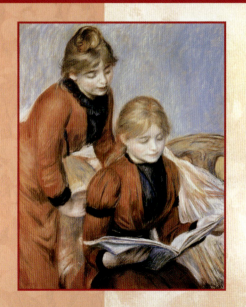

The best thing my sister gave me was the chance to learn from her mistakes.

DECEMBER 16

Sisters are great counselors because they know just what to say to make your heart lighter.

January 31

Sisters allow us the freedom to be totally, wholly, and unapologetically ourselves—if only because they know us so well we couldn't dare pretend to be anything but.

DECEMBER 15

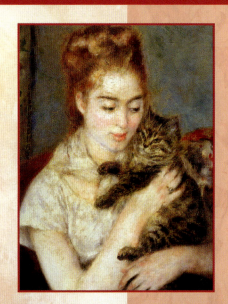

The creed of sisterhood: Give, and then give again. A sister is the one person certain to do the same.

FEBRUARY 1

Friends may come and go, but sisters are forever.

December 14

Side by side we spent our childhood
Sewn together at the seams.
And though we now lead separate lives,
We share the fabric of our dreams.

FEBRUARY 2

We were born ten minutes apart, Adrian first. She always said she was the real baby, and I was a kind of backup.

—ADAIR LARA, ON HER TWIN SISTER ADRIAN

December 13

When I was little, I prayed for snow days, for chocolate for dinner, and that we'd always be best friends.

FEBRUARY 3

When you have a loving sister, everything will come out all right.

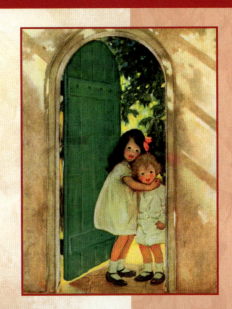

December 12

Take one angel. Remove wings and halo. Add equal parts devotion and compassion. Stir in friendship and a pinch of motherly concern. Mix well with wisdom and pour into mold marked "sister."

February 4

A sister loves us for ourselves; or rather, she loves us in spite of ourselves.

DECEMBER 11

As long as you're around, a little piece of my childhood is close at hand.

February 5

Sisters are connected at the heart. No amount of time or distance can break the bond between two people who share their lives, their hopes, and their dreams.

DECEMBER 10

Good counsel has no price.
—GIUSEPPE MAZZINI

FEBRUARY 6

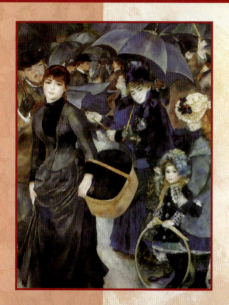

A sister's smile can brighten even the cloudiest day.

December 9

Sisters listen with their hearts and answer with their actions.

FEBRUARY 7

My sister taught me everything I need to know, and she was only in the sixth grade at the time.

—LINDA SUNSHINE

December 8

It's funny how the one person you hated sharing anything with as a child—your sister—is the person with whom you share everything as an adult.

FEBRUARY 8

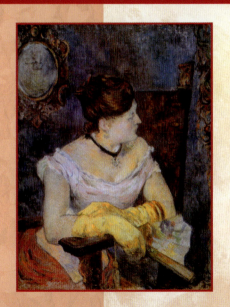

A sister is the person to whom you tell everything you could never tell your mom.

DECEMBER 7

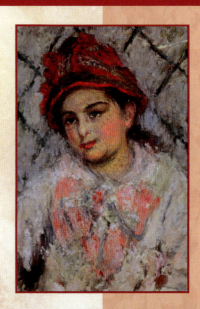

Sisters are the links in a chain. They hold you together and keep you strong, even when you are being pulled in all directions.

FEBRUARY 9

As time goes by, I realize more and more how much my sister means to me. She is part of my past, my present, and my future.

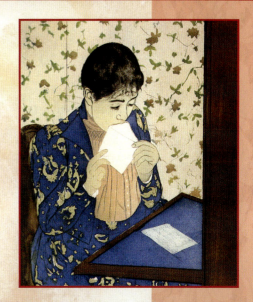

DECEMBER 6

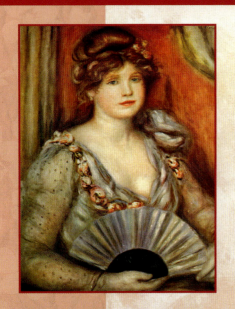

A sister is a forever friend.

—AMERICAN PROVERB

FEBRUARY 10

Sister, the best memories of my childhood always include you.

December 5

God made sisters for all those times when friends just don't come through for you.

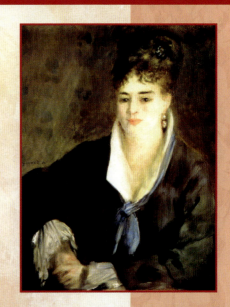

FEBRUARY 11

She may not be a famous actress or a powerful and important diplomat, but to me, my sister is a bright, shining star whose loving influence reaches into the lives of everyone she meets.

December 4

My sister! With that thrilling word
    Let thoughts unnumbered wildly spring!
What echoes in my heart are stirred,
    While thus I touch the trembling string.

—Margaret Davidson

FEBRUARY 12

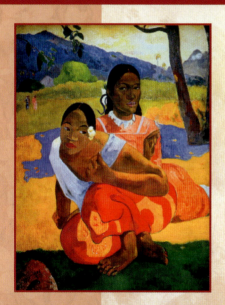

A sister is there to shout your joys and catch your tears.

December 3

I am at once buoyed and anchored by my sister.

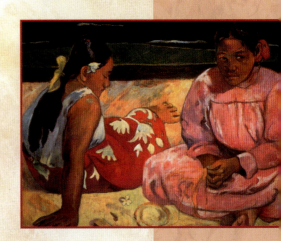

February 13

Complete agreement can be most satisfying, but sometimes it is the differences between two sisters that make for a marvelous adventure in friendship.

DECEMBER 2

Thank You, Sister

Thank you, sister, for helping me wise up without dampening my spirit.

FEBRUARY 14

It is through sisters that we learn about love.

DECEMBER 1

Friends will be there the first time.
Best friends will be there the
second time.
Sisters will be there *every* time.

FEBRUARY 15

A sister is our first roommate, our first playmate, and our first best friend.

November 30

When I thank God for the blessings in my life, you're at the top of the list.

FEBRUARY 16

A sister is the kind of friend who loves you enough to give you her last piece of chocolate.

NOVEMBER 29

With all beings and all things we shall be as relatives.

—SIOUX SAYING

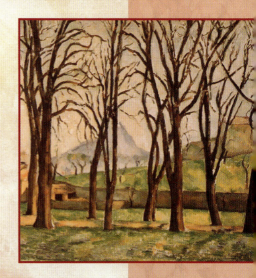

FEBRUARY 17

Help one another, is part of the religion of sisterhood.
—Louisa May Alcott

NOVEMBER 28

When sisters meet, they love to share new recipes, old stories, and lots of laughter.

FEBRUARY 18

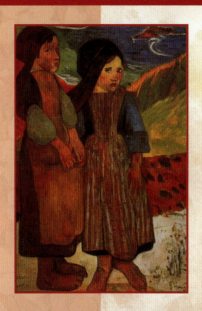

With or without a sister you will know sorrow, but with a sister you will never know it alone.

NOVEMBER 27

Each sister brings something different and delicious to the table reserved just for "family."

FEBRUARY 19

A sister will ask you how you are, and then actually listen to your answer.

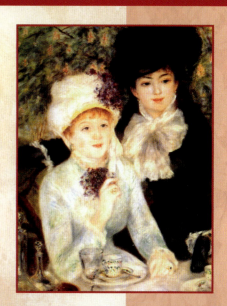

November 26

Not a day goes by when I don't thank the Lord for putting you in my life, sister. You mean more to me than you will ever truly know.

FEBRUARY 20

Life would be only half as much fun without my sister. Each time I see her smile or hear her cheery voice on the phone, my world suddenly seems twice as nice.

November 25

Sisters count on each other's strengths and compensate for each other's weaknesses.

FEBRUARY 21

When God sent me a sister, he must have interviewed every angel in heaven for the job.

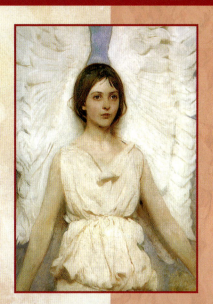

November 24

To have a sister is to have everything.

February 22

Sisters share a sense of humor that no one else is privy to. They speak a language of laughter that only they understand, a special code of joy that gives them the giggles whenever they are in each other's presence.

November 23

Sisters respect your position, even when they don't agree.

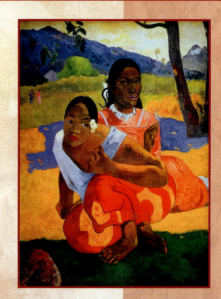

FEBRUARY 23

A sister's faith can help us believe we have the power to reach our highest goals.

November 22

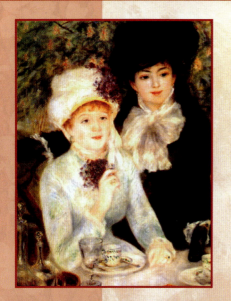

Having someone to share my life with is my definition of "sibling revelry." I cherish and celebrate my sister every day in every way.

FEBRUARY 24

Those who tease you, love you.

—JEWISH PROVERB

November 21

Through life's journey, a sister will walk beside you, cheer you on, give you a push, and even carry you when needed.

FEBRUARY 25

Sometimes life-changing plans are made by sisters when they are giggling and whispering under the covers.

November 20

Others might need to ask, "What's so funny?" Chances are your sister already knows and is laughing just as hard as you are.

FEBRUARY 26

No matter how much your sister loves you, she secretly wanted all your toys.

November 19

Biology is only a small part of what makes a woman a "sister."

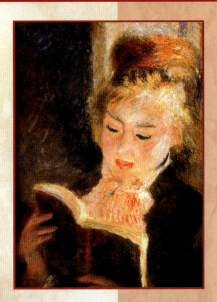

February 27

My sister knows the parts of our youth—the secret exploits and adventures our mom and dad never knew—that made us who we are.

NOVEMBER 18

In thy face, I see the map of honor, truth, and loyalty.

—WILLIAM SHAKESPEARE

February 28

My sister can bring sunlight into a room, dance among the stars, and hang the moon.

November 17

We may take different paths in life, but no matter where we go, we keep a little part of each other in our hearts.

FEBRUARY 29

A sister is as kind as she is wise
and as willing as she is able.

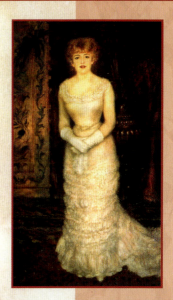

November 16

Sisters are cheaper than therapy and a lot more effective.

March 1

Having a sister isn't hard—not having one is!

November 15

My sister and I, you will recollect, were twins, and you know how subtle are the links which bind two souls which are so closely allied.
—Sir Arthur Conan Doyle

MARCH 2

With are comforted by the love that lies in the kindly depths of a sister's eye.

—PHOEBE CARY, "TO THE CHILDREN"

November 14

Sisters keep your secrets and tell you theirs.

MARCH 3

Like the gentle breeze that lifts the kite
    into the sky above,
My sister lifts me up and lets me
    soar on wings of love.

November 13

Sister:
When we were young,
You were the enemy
I had to love.
Now that we're older,
You're the friend
I love to have.

MARCH 4

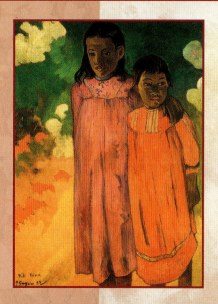

A sister is the absolute comfort of feeling entirely safe with a person.

November 12

Downtime with my sister? 100 percent uplifting!

MARCH 5

Sisters don't see one another with their eyes, they see with their hearts.

November 11

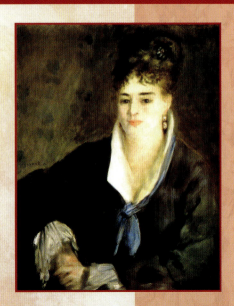

In my opinion, sisters are God's best invention yet.

MARCH 6

I *have* lost a treasure, such a Sister, such a friend, as never can have been surpassed—she was the sun of my life, the gilder of every pleasure, the soother of every sorrow, I had not a thought concealed from her, and it is as if I had lost a part of myself.

—CASSANDRA AUSTEN,
ON THE DEATH OF HER SISTER JANE

November 10

It's wonderful that with passing time your big sister mothers you less and confides in you more.

MARCH 7

When times are rough, sisters do small and unexpected things to change your whole perspective.

November 9

Sisters help us deal successfully with all the important firsts in our lives.

MARCH 8

For there is no friend like a sister
In calm or stormy weather;
To cheer one on the tedious way,
To fetch one if one goes astray,
To lift one if one totters down,
To strengthen whilst one stands.

—Christina Georgina Rossetti, "Goblin Market"

NOVEMBER 8

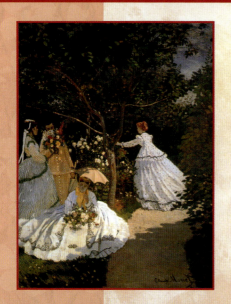

Like a ribbon of laughter through the years and the glittering of jewels gathered from far-off places are the memories of sisters.

MARCH 9

Sisters love to remind you over and over again how much wiser and more experienced they are at handling life's ups and downs. The problem is... they are usually right.

NOVEMBER 7

I don't believe beauty is only skin deep; I've seen it radiate from my sister's heart and soul.

MARCH 10

Two things that last forever: the memories and love I've shared with my sister.

November 6

A good sister will respond politely to an invitation, but she won't wait for one if she thinks you need her.

MARCH 11

Much as you may try, you can never legally divorce your sister. Consequently, you are stuck with this person for life.

—LINDA SUNSHINE, *MOM LOVES ME BEST (AND OTHER LIES YOUR SISTER TOLD YOU)*

November 5

Sisters are as beautiful as jewels but much more precious.

March 12

We may be as different on the outside as velvet and lace, but on the inside we are cut from the same cloth, woven from strands of loyalty and love.

November 4

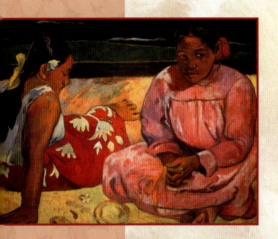

Although some things go without saying, a sister always finds the words.

MARCH 13

Thank You, Sister

Through life's storms and tempests, thank you for being my lighthouse.

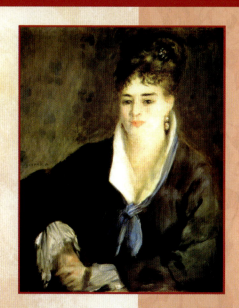

NOVEMBER 3

Thank You, Sister

Thank you, sister, for all the things you fix so lovingly and unselfishly.

MARCH 14

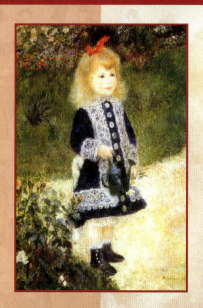

Big sister,
Thank you for letting me follow in your footsteps... and thank you for not expecting me to fill your shoes.

November 2

Children of the same family, the same blood, with the same first associations and habits, have some means of enjoyment in their power, which no subsequent connections can supply.

—Jane Austen, *Mansfield Park*

March 15

One of the best things about having a sister is knowing you'll always get an honest opinion.

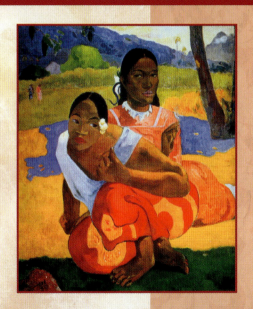

NOVEMBER 1

When this world is depressing
And my problems are distressing,
Sister, you are there—
What a blessing!

March 16

Friends may play walk-on roles in the stories of our lives. But sisters are the supporting leads, always there beside us to cheer us on as we stand in the spotlight.

October 31

Sisters share clothing, hair dryers, and bathrooms. They share laughter, friends, and lots of chocolate. And, in the end, they share a lifetime of memories.

March 17

Sisters don't count miles or years; they measure by the heart.

October 30

You know that you can have your say,
And she'll have her say, too.
But she will love you anyway,
And still be friends with you.

MARCH 18

Sisters come in perfectly matched sets and in intriguing assortments that make you think God has quite an eye for putting just the right mix together.

October 29

A sister will love you still, even when you feel you don't deserve it.

July 1

There came a time in my own life when it suddenly became clear to me that my sister was the one person who had known me for the longest time.

—Elizabeth Jolley, Australian essayist

July 16

Sisters are like seashells, snowflakes, and precious works of art: each is a unique and beautiful treasure that can never be duplicated or replaced.

July 2

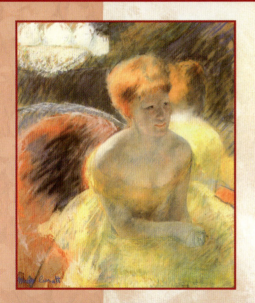

A sister loves you like you should love yourself.

July 15

When in doubt, I call my sister. She always knows just the right answer to any question. When in fear, I call my sister. She always has just the right words of comfort to make me feel strong and secure.

July 3

There is real power in sisterhood. It can transform ages and dissolve distance.

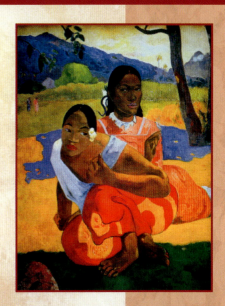

JULY 14

If Cassandra were going to have her head cut off, Jane would insist on sharing her fate.

—ATTRIBUTED TO CASSANDRA AUSTEN, MOTHER OF JANE AUSTEN AND HER SISTER CASSANDRA

July 4

Monday July 4th.
Dearest Arabel's birthday. She is 18; and an interesting, intelligent, amiable feeling girl. I should love her even if she were not my sister; and even if she did not love me.

—Elizabeth Barrett (Browning) writing in her diary about her sister Arabella on July 4, 1831

July 13

Thank You, Sister

Thank you for laughing at my jokes, wiping my tears, and supporting me in everything I do.

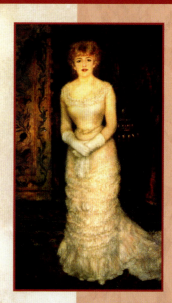

July 5

If you would choose your sister as a friend—even if she weren't your sister—then both you and your sister are blessed.

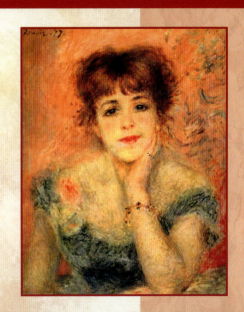

July 12

We go together like
Tea and crumpets,
Milk and cookies,
Chicken and dumplings,
Sweet and sour,
Chocolate and milk,
Apples and cinnamon,
Satin and silk.
We go together like
Sand and sea,
The perfect combination,
My sister and me.

JULY 6

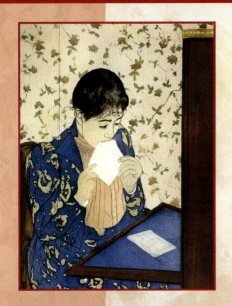

A kind word from my sister is like a hug across the miles.

July 11

You don't always have to like your sister, but you love her nonetheless. Even when you are at each other's throats, you are in each other's hearts.

July 7

People who believe that boys are more competitive than girls have never seen sisters trying to get ready at the same time in the same bathroom.

July 10

Sister, I am honored to be yours.

July 8

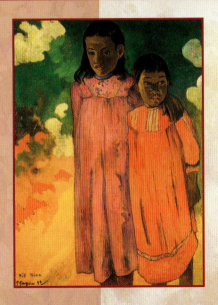

Being sisters is no accident.
It is the divine will of God.

July 9

You are more than my sister.
You are a friend, a companion,
A keeper of memories and
A reservoir of who I was and what
I am becoming.

July 17

Even if she dislikes it, your sister will defend your choice of bridesmaids' dresses.

June 30

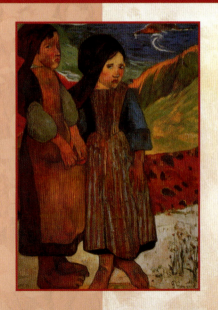

No matter our differences, we can always agree on this: Our love for each other can see us through any disagreements.

July 18

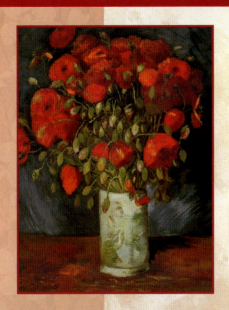

There is no problem on earth that a sister and a pound of chocolate can't cure!

June 29

Thank You, Sister

I have learned most of what I know from watching you.

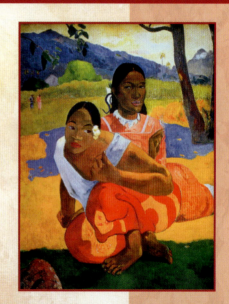

July 19

I feel sad for people who have only brothers. To live life without a sister is to miss out on a special kind of happiness.

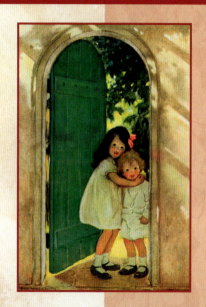

June 28

Whether she is loaning me money, lending me clothes, or giving me advice, my sister is the most generous soul I know.

July 20

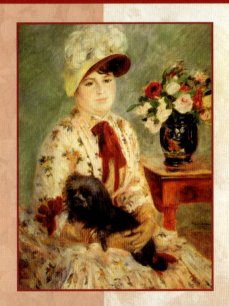

The true hallmark of a sister is that she knows all about you and loves you anyway.

June 27

Most girls know that whenever they are missing a favorite dress, they can usually find it in their sister's closet.

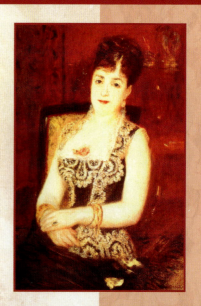

July 21

Have faith in God and family. Both are forever on your side.

June 26

God blessed us with sisters so we'd have a constant source of clothes to borrow, stories to swap, shoulders to lean on, and feelings to share.

July 22

Thank You, God

Thank God for sisters who love you enough to tell you when you are acting like an idiot. That kind of honesty is rarely found even among friends.

June 25

A sister is the person who can finish your sentences, yet conversations still manage to go on for hours!

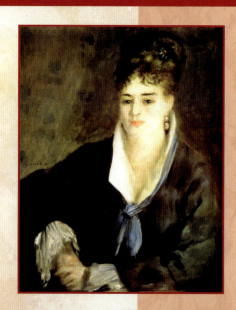

July 23

Of course you take your sister for granted. That's one of the beauties of the relationship.

June 24

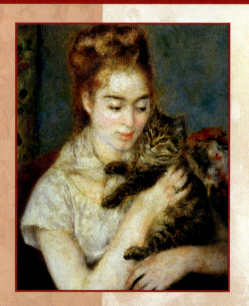

I know my sister is beautiful inside as well as out, for I have seen her heart.

JULY 24

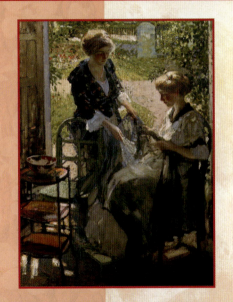

My sister... is my sounding board, my confidante, my keeper of secrets—and my best friend.

—KATHLEEN O'KEEFE

June 23

A sister's hug wraps you in the love and security of the home where you grew up.

July 25

Sisters are the people from whom we learn how and how *not*—ouch!—to treat others.

June 22

Parents give you life.
Sisters walk you through it.

JULY 26

That same sister who claimed she wasn't strong enough to bring the vacuum upstairs would move mountains to help you.

June 21

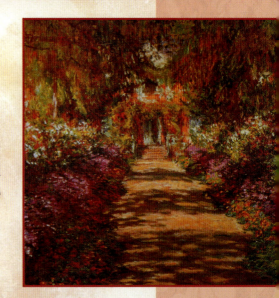

With the gift of listening comes the gift of healing.

—Catherine de Hueck Doherty, *Poustinia*

July 27

Sisters needn't speak to communicate, for the language of sisters is more than mere words.

June 20

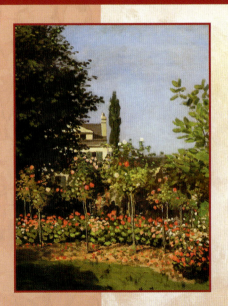

An honest answer is the sign of true friendship.

—Unknown

July 28

We may not always agree on things,
And we often fuss and fight.
But having my sister beside me
Makes everything turn out all right.

June 19

Sisters are like pearls... precious, imperfect, and beautiful.

July 29

No problem is so bad and no joy so great that it can't be made better by sharing it with a sister.

June 18

Once we were constantly in each other's hair, always pulling and tugging and twisting. Now we are constantly in each other's hair, only this time it's styling, coloring, trimming, and highlighting!

July 30

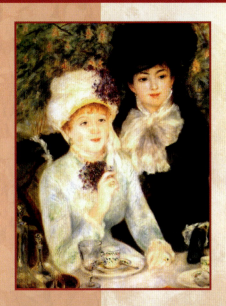

A sister is someone you can always talk to. She will tell it like it is, say what needs to be said, and maybe even listen.

June 17

I felt it shelter to speak to you.
—Emily Dickinson

July 31

I am so thankful for my best friend. Not only is she my best friend, she is also my sister.

June 16

God created sisters from the finest of materials, shaping them to perfection with loving hands. Each one is a priceless and unique masterpiece.

August 1

Your sister is your other self.

—Barbara Mathias,
Between Sisters

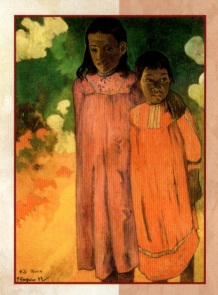

June 15

Thank You, Sister

Thank you for the times you've led me places I wouldn't otherwise go, held my hand as we walked, and stood behind me when I faltered.

AUGUST 2

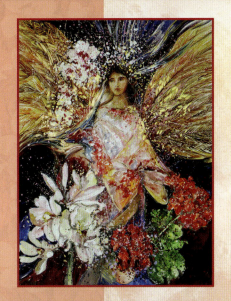

How is it that I know my sister was meant for me? The same way I know God hears me and angels fly— I simply believe.

June 14

No matter how far apart we live, my sister and I feel close to each other. The life we've shared and the love we hold in our hearts keep us connected across the miles.

AUGUST 3

Sisters know the true meaning of conspiracy.

June 13

Little sisters follow you constantly, imitate your every move, and are forever getting into all your things—including your heart.

AUGUST 4

We cannot destroy kindred: Our chains stretch a little sometimes, but they never break.

—MARIE DE RABUTIN-CHANTAL, MARQUISE DE SÉVIGNÉ, *LETTERS OF MADAME DE SÉVIGNÉ TO HER DAUGHTER AND HER FRIENDS*, VOL. 1

June 12

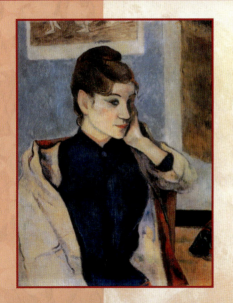

Thank You, Sister

Thank you for being the one person I can trust with anything and everything.

AUGUST 5

The road between sisters is short, straight, and paved with flowers.

June 11

Sisters keep you honest. It's hard to put on airs around someone who has seen you at your absolute worst.

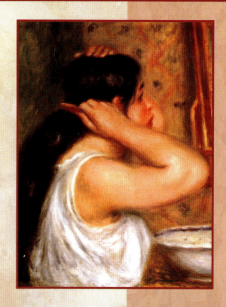

August 6

Two sisters have a special bond
   impossible to sever.
It keeps them close in heart and mind—
   the best of friends forever.

June 10

Thank You, God

She may sometimes drive me crazy, get on my nerves, and tax my spirit, but she is always my best friend. She is my sister, and I thank God for her presence in my life.

AUGUST 7

Thank You, Sister

You know my most embarrassing moments and love me anyway.

June 9

Sometimes we achieve our childhood dreams simply because we told our sister we would.

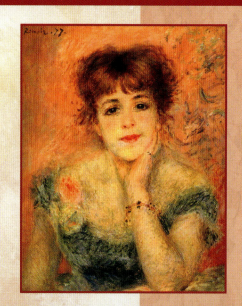

August 8

We don't see eye to eye on things
    like politics or God,
But when it comes to having fun,
    we're two peas in a pod.

June 8

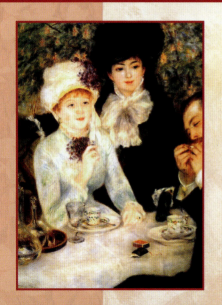

Husbands come and go; children come and eventually go. Friends grow up and move away. But the one thing that's never lost is your sister.

—Gail Sheehy

August 9

A sister's consistent kindness is a star in the darkness of night.

June 7

We've had our ups and downs and bumpy patches—but I'm sure glad I'm on the ride with you, sister!

AUGUST 10

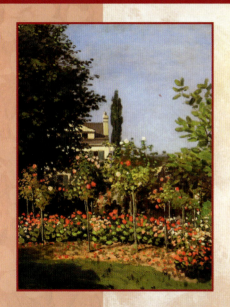

We are rich only through what we give, and poor only through what we refuse.

—ANNE SOPHIE SWETCHINE,
THE WRITINGS OF MADAME SWETCHINE

June 6

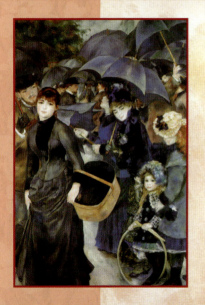

Whether you have one sister or seven, it is never a sister too many.

August 11

Sisters nurture each other's hearts like the Good Shepherd tends his flock.

June 5

Oh, the comfort—the inexpressible comfort of feeling *safe* with a person—having neither to weigh thoughts nor measure words, but pouring them all right out, just as they are, chaff and grain together; certain that a faithful hand will take and sift them, keep what is worth keeping, and then with the breath of kindness blow the rest away.

—Dinah Maria Mulock Craik, *A Life for a Life*

AUGUST 12

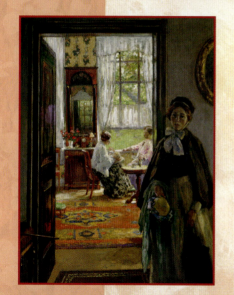

Reconnecting with a sister
After time or miles divide,
Is like opening the door
Of a favorite place—
And being welcomed inside.

June 4

One good thing about having a sister is that the question of who's going to be your maid of honor was answered the minute she was born.

August 13

The Lord has blessed me with someone
    on whom I can depend,
And given me the gift of both
    a sister and a friend.

June 3

Sisterhood is friendship elevated to art.

August 14

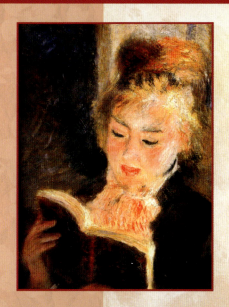

A trusted sister is the keeper of our secret dreams.

June 2

Sisters are always drying their hair.
Locked into rooms, alone,
They pose at the mirror, shoulders bare,
Trying this way and that their hair,
Or fly importunate down the stair
To answer the telephone.

—Phyllis McGinley

August 15

There's a simple kind of freedom sisters enjoy. Freedom to share innermost thoughts, to ask favors, to show true feelings. The freedom to simply be themselves.

JUNE 1

A sister is never farther away than needing her can reach.

August 16

Thank You, Sister

Thank you for always being the kind of person who I am proud to call my sister.

MAY 31

Hope is recognizing God's face behind those of family and friends as they accompany us through life's valleys.

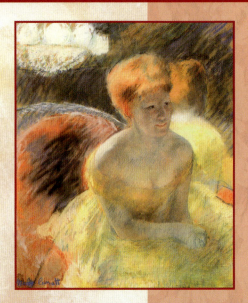

August 17

The sun shines brighter in the company of a sister. The road stretches out across the horizon. Adventures lie before the two of you that would never be taken alone.

May 30

She shares good times and bad, secrets and laughter, joy and despair. A sister is someone who sticks by your side no matter what challenges life tosses in your direction.

August 18

It wouldn't have been like my sister to throw her arms around me the day our mother died... She offered me the one promise she could wholeheartedly make. "I'm the only one now who remembers the day of your birth," she told me. "No matter what, I will always be your sister."

—Joyce Maynard, on her sister Rona

May 29

A sister forgives you when you have to cancel at the last minute.

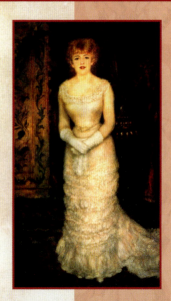

AUGUST 19

One good sister is worth a hundred friends.

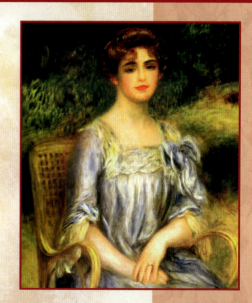

MAY 28

Sisters are as close as hands and feet.
—VIETNAMESE PROVERB

August 20

I can't even count how many fights started because, "She's looking at me!" Now I only wish we had that much time to spend together.

May 27

Thank You, Sister

For all the times you kept me safe from harm, I thank you. For all the ways you guided me toward what was best for me, I thank you. For all the love you've given me, I thank you most of all.

AUGUST 21

A sister is a gift from God, sent from above to make life worthwhile here below.

—ANONYMOUS

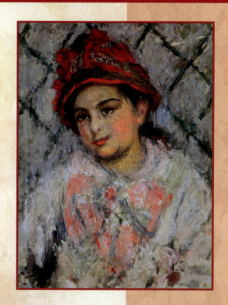

May 26

Time passes.
Children grow up.
Careers end.
Friends forget.
Love fades.
Sisters remain.

August 22

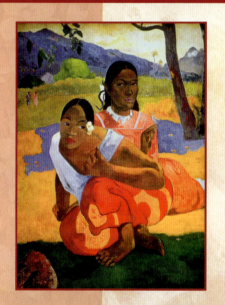

It doesn't matter whether or not we had similar interests or lifestyles. We learned to love each other as children, and we never stopped.

—Mary Binney Montgomery

MAY 25

When God made sisters, he doubled the love and then poured an extra batch of caring and compassion into the mold.

AUGUST 23

Sisters are two individual beings joined together at the hip and the heart.

MAY 24

Friendships bloom
And friendships end,
But a sister is
An eternal best friend.

August 24

Sibling Withdrawal Syndrome

noun: a state of melancholy resulting from lack of time spent with one's sister.

MAY 23

It's funny how in always walking beside me you taught me how to stand on my own.

AUGUST 25

My sisters have always been my best friends. As other friendships faded with the end of a school year or sports season, my sisters remained. When relationships exploded in a firestorm of words or collapsed amid a torrent of tears, my sisters endured.

MAY 22

The harmony between sisters is a wondrous thing.

AUGUST 26

It takes a great listener to be a great sister.

May 21

Time spins a golden thread through the tightly woven fabric of sisterhood.

AUGUST 27

Don't mind if your sister's not overly impressed with your latest accomplishments. She just never expected anything less.

MAY 20

As a kid, I hated it when people mistook me for you. Now I consider it a compliment!

August 28

Sisters are treasures, but they are also treasure chests, eternal keepers of our richest secrets and dreams.

MAY 19

Even when sisters take different paths they walk the road of life hand in hand.

August 29

Thank You, Sister

If I had been an only child, I might have had more toys, nicer clothes, and all of the attention. But nothing could replace what I would have missed—You!

May 18

A sister may look like you, sound like you, and think like you. Or, she might be your polar opposite. But she's still a part of you, a very special kind of double.

August 30

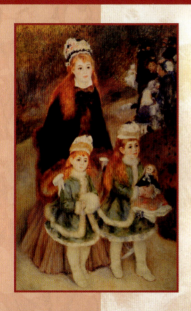

Sisters do not have to be twins to be twin souls.

May 17

Time and distance may separate my sister and me, but they will never come between us.

AUGUST 31

Sisters need not be cut from the same cloth to be bound by common thread.

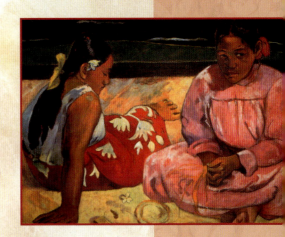

MAY 16

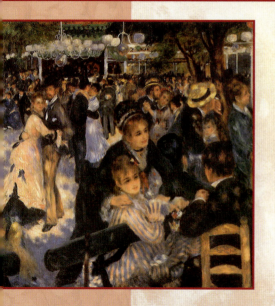

The only thing better than having a loving, supportive sister is being one myself.

September 1

One of the miracles of sisters is that they can grow separately without growing apart.

May 15

I used to tell on my sister.
Now I tell her everything.

September 2

You express me better than I express myself.

—Walt Whitman,
"Song of the Open Road"

May 14

When I think back to the good ol' days, who is the one person I inevitably picture? My sister.

September 3

You and I, we share the title of
Sister, and yes, we are much the same.
We have the same hair, and similar eyes,
Unfortunately, we have the same thighs.
But whether we share our secrets or our hair,
I'm grateful that being sisters is
    something we share.

May 13

Thank You, Sister

You've shown me so often how much you love me and care for me. For every one of those times, thanks a million.

SEPTEMBER 4

Thank You, Sister

When I'm with you, I feel certain I am making the most of every moment.

May 12

God gave me two shoulders to carry burdens, a creative mind to figure out solutions, and a strong heart to weather disappointments. And I have yet one more tool to successfully face anything this world can throw my way: God gave me my sister.

SEPTEMBER 5

You can depend on your sister for perspective when your own vision gets out of focus.

May 11

No matter their age, sisters keep each other young at heart and in spirit.

September 6

There's no instruction manual for how to be a sister. Like laughter, it comes naturally.

May 10

"My sister." I say it with pride, as if I had something to do with it.

September 7

There's a special place in heaven reserved just for sisters.

May 9

We can sing like superstars and dance like we're famous.
We can stay in our PJs all day and eat right out of the ice-cream container.
With you, sister, there is no pretense, no show.
I am safe just being myself.

September 8

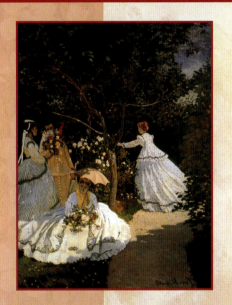

My sisters have been my safety nets, my life jackets, and the sources of so many discoveries and joys in my life.

—Carol Wincenc

MAY 8

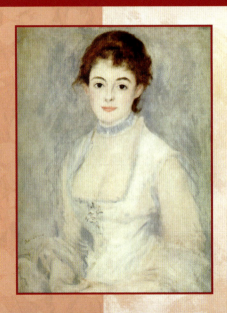

A sister is there to share your joy and suffering alike.

SEPTEMBER 9

Thank You, Sister

I admire your heart, your humor, your kindness, and your talents. You are the role model Mom always hoped I'd have.

MAY 7

When we were in school, I did everything I could to avoid being with my "uncool" sister. Now I go out of my way to spend as much time with her as I can. And I even think she's cool.

SEPTEMBER 10

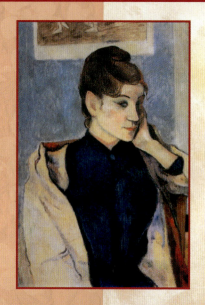

Sisterhood is made up of layer upon layer of little memories.

May 6

Thank You, Sister

Thank you for choosing me to be the person with whom you share your successes, your failures, your happiness, and your heartbreak.

September 11

Blood's thicker than water, and when one's in trouble, best to seek out a relative's open arms.

—Euripides

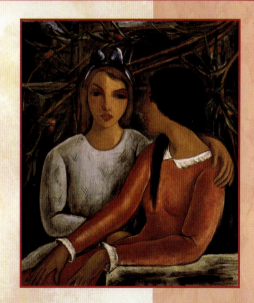

May 5

Sisters are angels with familiar faces.

SEPTEMBER 12

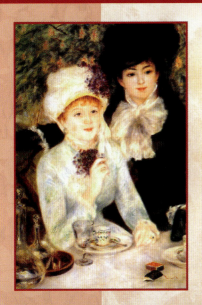

On the tennis court of life, I can't think of anyone I'd rather play doubles with than my sister.

May 4

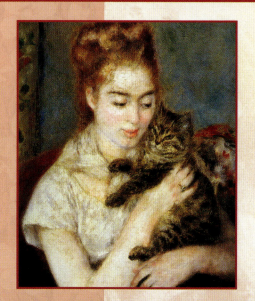

If only your sister's closet were as big as her heart!

SEPTEMBER 13

We are thy sisters...
Our skins may differ, but from thee we claim
A sister's privilege and a sister's name.

—SARAH L. FORTEN

May 3

As we pass through the phases of our lives, developing or strengthening parts of our personalities, we lose certain friends along the way. But those who travel with us, sharing our personal journeys and reveling in our private growth, are much more than friends. They are our sisters.

September 14

Everywhere, we learn only from those we love.
—Johann Wolfgang von Goethe

May 2

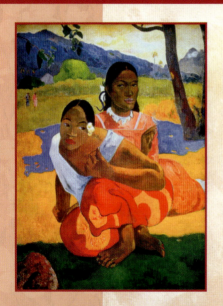

I'm even grateful for the times we didn't get along, sister. They taught me how love and patience can mend any rift.

SEPTEMBER 15

A sister is someone you don't have to see or talk to every day. The bond of sisterhood is strong enough to outlast any amount of time or distance.

May 1

So brothers and sisters, as we go, still let us move as one.
—Alice Cary

SEPTEMBER 16

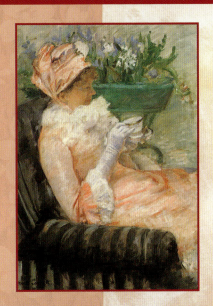

Not quite a mom, more than a friend, so much like myself— my sister.

April 30

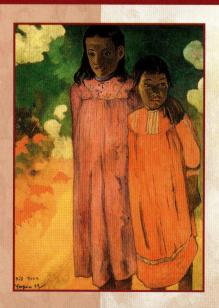

A sister is more precious than an eye.

—Barbara Kingsolver,
Animal Dreams

SEPTEMBER 17

Sisters are for giggles and secrets while they are young and for comfort and assurance in old age.

April 29

Thank You, God

Thank you, God, for giving me the kind of sister who tells it like it is, gives it to me straight, and takes me just the way I am.

September 18

Families are circles of love in which no one wants to be the first to let go of someone else's hand.

April 28

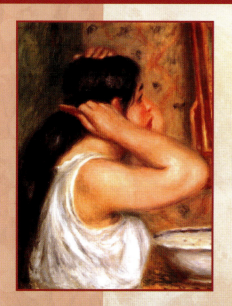

My sister is the person who knows me better than I know myself.

SEPTEMBER 19

Thank You, God

Thank you, God, for my sister, who knows me better than anyone else, yet never holds it against me.

APRIL 27

Sisters make other "best friends" seem slightly less "best."

SEPTEMBER 20

My sister is a shining example of the strength family members can give each other.

April 26

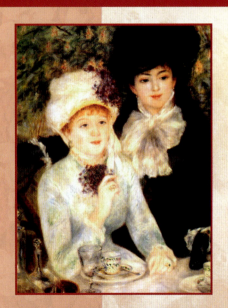

As a child I wanted to be more like you. Know what? I still do.

SEPTEMBER 21

God has given us the capacity to achieve great things, as well as a sister for moral support along the way.

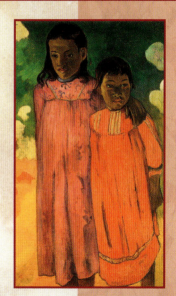

April 25

Sisters return things to the store for you when you're too embarrassed to do it.

SEPTEMBER 22

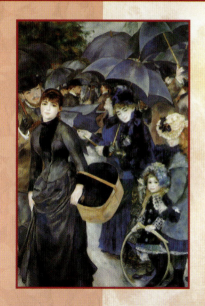

Sisters function as safety nets in a chaotic world simply by being there for each other.
—CAROL SALINE, *SISTERS*

APRIL 24

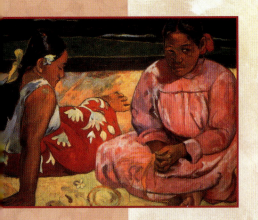

Thank You, Sister

We haven't had the easiest of lives, but I think we've made the rough times better by facing them together.

SEPTEMBER 23

Thank You, Sister

What sunshine is to flowers, you are to my heart. Thank you for always nurturing me.

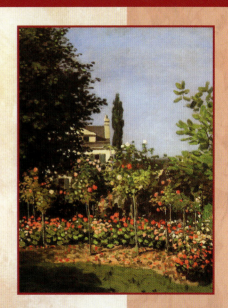

April 23

When you forget who you truly are, you can count on your sister to remind you.

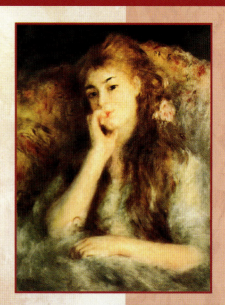

SEPTEMBER 24

"You remind me of your sister" is the greatest compliment ever bestowed.

APRIL 22

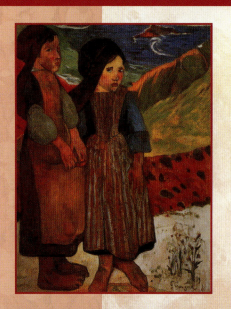

God made sisters unique enough to be individuals, yet similar enough to be the best of friends.

SEPTEMBER 25

A house full of sisters is always endearing... and rarely quiet.

APRIL 21

In times of test, family is best.
—BURMESE SAYING

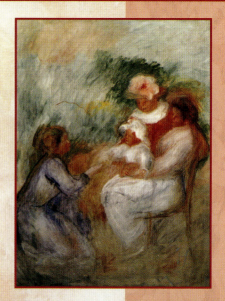

SEPTEMBER 26

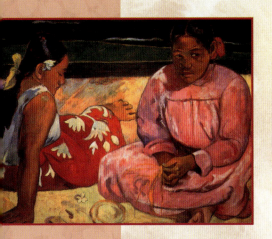

Even the silence between sisters is comfortable.

April 20

Thank You, Sister

You held my hand when I was frightened by a nightmare. You walked me to school when I was scared and uncertain. You played with me when my friends were not around. Thanks, sis, for always being so kind and warm and giving.

SEPTEMBER 27

She knows your biggest fear, your fondest wish, and your most embarrassing moment—but, of course, you know all that about her as well.

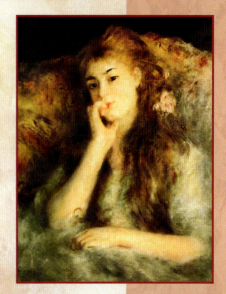

APRIL 19

I can tell my sister anything and trust she will keep every secret.

SEPTEMBER 28

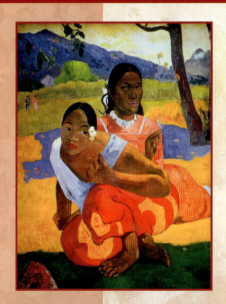

Sisters in our hearts, sisters in our souls—sisters forever.

APRIL 18

Through years of practice, sisters learn to dance without stepping on each other's toes.

SEPTEMBER 29

If the length of a friendship is the measure of its strength, I can have no better friend than my sister.

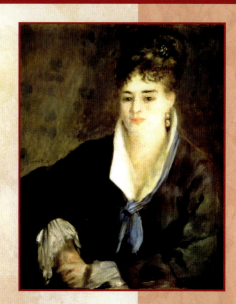

April 17

Love defies any distance that might separate sisters.

SEPTEMBER 30

Thank you for all the times you looked so I could leap.

APRIL 16

Sisters are
Wish-upon-a-star,
Cross-your-heart and hope-to-die,
Deepest, darkest secrets,
Good times and bad times,
Borrow anything,
Tell you everything,
Always and forever.

October 1

A sister's heart is a well of love, never depleted, at the bottom of which lies forgiveness.

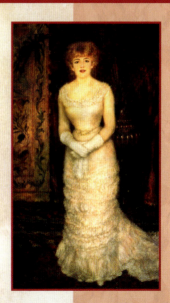

April 15

God made us sisters;
hearts made us friends.
—AMERICAN SAYING

OCTOBER 2

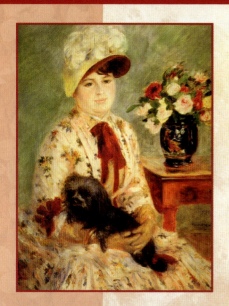

A sister is someone who knows all your deepest, darkest secrets and loves you anyway.

April 14

Sisters are the bridges that help us reach other shores when troubled waters roil between.

October 3

A quarrel between sisters, after it passes, makes their bond even stronger.

April 13

Miles can't separate sisters; neither can years. They are always, at some level, connected.

October 4

How do people make it through life without a sister?
—Sara Corpening

APRIL 12

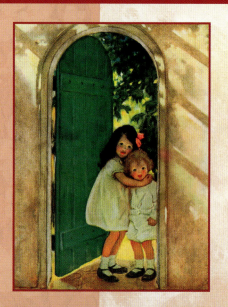

When my sister hugs me, it feels as though I am wrapped in the wings of an angel.

OCTOBER 5

Thank You, Sister

I may not always remember to tell you how much you mean to me, but I think of it every day.

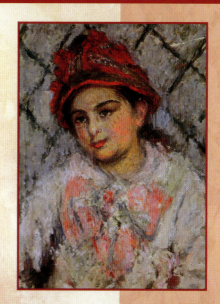

April 11

You know full well as I do the value of sisters' affections to each other; there is nothing like it in this world.

—Charlotte Brontë

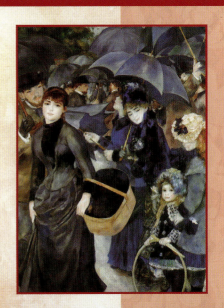

October 6

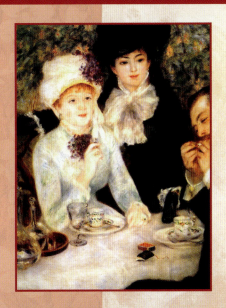

Lord help the mister
Who comes between me
and my sister.

—Irving Berlin, "Sisters"

April 10

The bond that links sisters is not merely blood. It comprises mutual respect, appreciation of differences, tolerance for weaknesses, and joy in each others' lives.

October 7

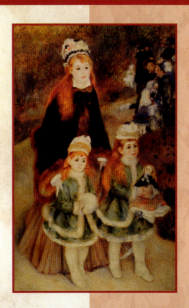

Little sisters are happy that someone is blazing the trail ahead; big sisters are comforted that someone is always close behind.

April 9

My sister is a blessing. Without her, who could I have blamed when something got broken?

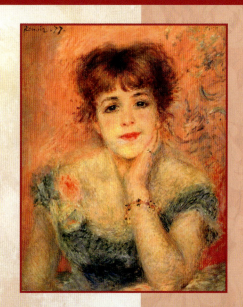

OCTOBER 8

When I am with my sister I feel that I am brilliant, beautiful, and interesting—if only because the person of whom I think the same is choosing to be with me.

April 8

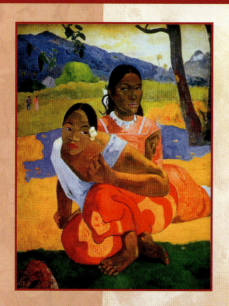

I once wanted to be just like my sister. Now I appreciate her for all the ways she and I are different, as well as for all the ways we are alike.

OCTOBER 9

The family—that dear octopus from whose tentacles we never quite escape, nor, in our inmost hearts, ever quite wish to.
—DODIE SMITH, *DEAR OCTOPUS*

April 7

Some sisters are steady, like the stars. Others are like flowers, opening slowly to reveal their wonder.

October 10

Hand in hand,
We walk together,
Heart to heart...
Friends forever.

April 6

Sisters make growing up more fun.

October 11

Jobs, boyfriends, hemlines, and hairstyles may come and go, but a sister lasts forever.

April 5

A sister is the best friend you didn't choose and didn't ask for but could never live without.

October 12

There are certain things in life on which we can depend: The sun will come up tomorrow, the grass will grow, and sisters will always, in the end, forgive one another.

April 4

I look into my sister's eyes and see a reflection of myself. I hear my sister laugh and feel her joy rise within my own heart.

October 13

Although you often know a faster path, you're always willing to walk a bit longer to keep me company.

April 3

What's the point of life if you can't share it with a sister?

OCTOBER 14

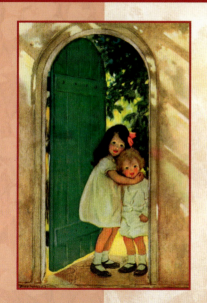

An only child believes that she isn't missing anything by not having sisters. It's just as well that she never will know better.

April 2

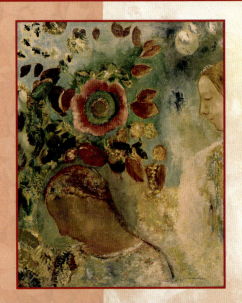

My sister and I are like flowers, growing separately, yet rooted in the same common ground.

OCTOBER 15

Sister, every time I've called you crying, I've hung up smiling.

April 1

I was eighteen months old when Susan was born. I don't think I've ever forgiven her for upstaging my solo act.

—LINDA SUNSHINE, *MOM LOVES ME BEST (AND OTHER LIES YOUR SISTER TOLD YOU)*

October 16

It isn't always easy having a sister. That's why God is so selective in choosing the one for us that makes the difficult times worthwhile.

MARCH 31

Sharing is at the heart of sisterhood—first rooms and secrets, then hopes, hearts, and all that you have to give.

October 17

To get the full value of joy you must have someone to divide it with.

—Mark Twain

MARCH 30

Having a sister is not only a gift but also a privilege.

October 18

Talking to your sister is like paging through a scrapbook of your life. All the memories are there, just waiting to be rediscovered.

March 29

Thank You, God

Thank you, God, for giving my sister strong shoulders for me to lean on, wisdom for me to learn from, and a joyful spirit for me to laugh with.

October 19

I don't know what lies ahead on the road I follow, but I know you will be there to take the journey with me.

March 28

No other love can quite compare to the special closeness sisters share.

—Anonymous

OCTOBER 20

Sisters stand between one and life's cruel circumstances.
—NANCY MITFORD

March 27

Into every life a little rain must fall. But it is only the luckiest among us who can take shelter in the arms of a sister.

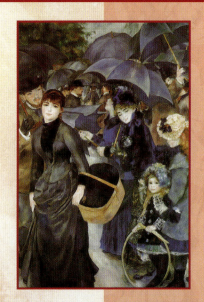

October 21

Home is never farther than a sister's smile.

MARCH 26

A sister knows your true shoe size, dress size, hair color, and, most important, the things that touch your heart.

October 22

Don't regret the fights you've had with your sister. It is those fights that have reminded you how much you stood to lose.

MARCH 25

I am grateful for all the blessings in my life, and one of the greatest is my sister.

October 23

Sometimes the only difference between a sister and a guardian angel is the wings.

MARCH 24

For better or for worse, you can rely on your sister to remind you who you truly are.

October 24

Sisters make each other laugh with a single word or a simple look or touch.

MARCH 23

Am I not a woman and a sister?
—ANTISLAVERY MOTTO

OCTOBER 25

It's not always easy being a sister; but then, the best things in life usually aren't.

MARCH 22

The best friend you will ever have is the first friend you ever made—your sister.

October 26

Thank You, Sister

There are no such things as "secrets" between sisters because the bond between them is too secure. A wish for a doll. Worries over grades. A first kiss. Concern for the future. How many times have we shared such issues with fear in our hearts, only to realize later that the problems were as fleeting as a heartbeat? Thank you for keeping my secrets over the years, Sis.

MARCH 21

Sisters are like wildflowers; they bloom generously in rocky places.

OCTOBER 27

Sisters love each other unconditionally.

March 20

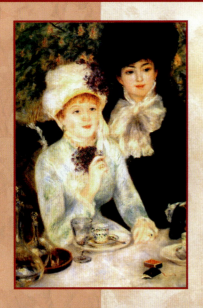

A sister is a kindred spirit in whom you can confide your soul.

October 28

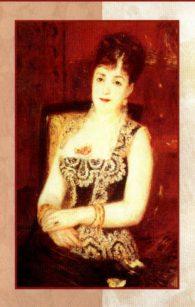

If I could choose the perfect sister
Who's everything I'm not,
I think when all is said and done
I'd keep the one I got.

MARCH 19

Thank You, Sister

Thank you for the times you've lent me your ear, your shoulder, your clothes....